The Archaeology of Peace

Jim O'Brien
1944–1994

Also By Jim O'Brien

*Maxims From Within
Connections*

The Archaeology of Peace – Original ink drawing
by Ray McManus, 2001

The Archaeology of Peace

Jim O'Brien

THE GOLDEN EAGLE PRESS
2008

www.thegoldeneaglepress.com

Copyright © 2008 James and Ruth E. O'Brien.

All rights reserved.

ISBN:0-615-25479-9
ISBN-13:9780615254791

Library of Congress Control Number: 2008908442

Visit www.booksurge.com to order additional copies.

First Edition, The Golden Eagle Press, 2008

Cover design by Rajesh Maurya

Title Page drawing, "The Archaeology of Peace," by Ray McManus

No part of this book may be reproduced in any manner without the express written consent of The Golden Eagle Press.

*This book is dedicated to Jonathon,
the torch bearer.*

TABLE OF CONTENTS

✤ ✤ ✤

Forward XI

Preface XV

Acknowledgements XIX

Philosophy 1

War and Justification 5

The Argument 9

Freedom 13

Truth 17

Reason 21

Strangeness 25

Peace 29

Uniqueness 33

Government 37

Intervention 63

Communication 69

References 83

FORWARD

Jim was my friend. And his untimely death in 1994 left behind his loving wife Ruth and his son (of whom he was inordinately proud). He also left behind his interlocutors, like me, who would often gather at his home for philosophical discussion and, given our individual perspectives, a lot of argument.

The pages of this, his last, book contain his reflections on the implications of a philosophy that celebrates the rational life: one in which each human being is accorded virtually absolute freedom and whose uniqueness is valued; one that accepts the "strangeness" in others, but, most significantly, values the freedom to think, to act, to live a life of one's own choosing. Underlying this vision lay a deeper passion: respect for all life and the unique history and trajectory through space-time of all life. In this regard, his revulsion at war as an absolute evil (with some exceptions) is directly related to his concept of a rational society, because it denies, and in his words, "crushes" human freedom. His is, I would argue, a utopian vision—something to strive to approximate whilst knowing that it cannot, given the variety of personalities and dispositions of our fellow human beings and the conflicts such variation inevitably produces.

As a friend and one who used to engage in lively, spirited, and sometimes contentious debate with Jim, I would like to honor his life by raising a question that is not addressed in this little book of big ideas and profound insight.

Jim held that all human beings should be accorded freedom; indeed, not to do so is, he believed, immoral. I have a tragic and personal reason to disagree with this in special cases, as when a person has what is labeled an "axis I mental disorder," such as schizophrenia, to name but one. In my own case, I have a daughter who is a paranoid schizophrenic who was never drug compliant. After having desisted from taking her medicine last year, she had a psychotic attack. As a result her husband is dead, and she will be confined to a mental hospital for perhaps the remainder of her life. This is a situation that clearly legitimates the restriction of personal freedom. Other cases involve sociopaths, people without conscience, who can do great harm (like Ted Bundy) and feel absolutely no remorse. Should they be allowed total personal freedom? I would have argued this with Jim, and he may have disagreed. But he would have respected my view, and we would have gone on to other philosophical problems of mutual interest.

There is a quote from John Milton's Areopagitica that seems appropriate to Jim's book (which, I would venture to guess, was destined to be his doctoral dissertation in philosophy, and which became, in his words "his contribution to rational thought"):

> *Where there is much desire to learn, there of necessity will be much arguing, much writing, many opinions; for opinion in good men is but knowledge in the making.*

Richard Magee
Los Cruces, New Mexico
November 2, 2008

PREFACE

Jim O'Brien was a man who spent a good deal of his life trying to live his own ideals and beliefs. He was a thinking man, one who revered logic and thought and strove to seek wisdom through those two paradigms. He had a thirst for knowledge, of the world around him and the world within—not just for the sake of seeking; Jim loved playing with the treasures of his internal and external wilderness forays and creating new ideas, new solutions for eternal human problems: transformations of thought into action—Jim O'Brien delighted in creating order out of our chaos.

The Archaeology of Peace has taken nearly fifteen years to publish. The writing took place as a result of a challenge I made to Jim in 1991 during the Persian Gulf War. "Why doesn't anyone write about peace? Why doesn't anyone figure out why we can't put a stop to wars?" *The Archaeology of Peace* was Jim's answer to those questions, his attempt to lead us in the direction of creating order out of our current chaos.

To find his answer, Jim began an archaeological dig to the core of our human existence—how we think and how our thoughts lead us to action. He used a lens of logical analysis to focus on who we humans are, the purpose of governments, the nature of freedom, and how we perceive self-defense. In the end, Jim challenges each of us to consider the way we think, how we as a species came to perceive our realities and identities, and with our free will, how to re-create our unexamined paradigms into a more humane and logical model for peaceful coexistence.

Whether or not the *Archaeology of Peace* was destined to evolve into a more expansive treatise on freedom befitting Jim's doctoral dissertation, we will never know. Though concise in pages, Jim considered this book a complete thought. Perhaps someday this smaller golden glimmer of truth and wisdom that he has left us will be spun into a golden thread, then woven into the tapestry of a more authentic and moral co-existence on this beautiful terra firma we call mother earth.

Ruth E. O'Brien
January 16, 2009
Oak Park, Illinois

ACKNOWLEDGEMENTS

The birth of this book could not have occurred without the incredible love and unwavering support of the following people.

Dr. Sherman M. Stanage, former chairman of the Philosophy Department at Northern Illinois University, was Jim's most respected and distinguished friend and mentor. Dr. Stanage inspired Jim to think authentically, to question relentlessly, and to seek knowledge and wisdom. Dr. Stanage motivated Jim to return to school where he entered the doctoral program under Stanage's tutelage. Dr. Stanage encouraged Jim's inquisitive mind and his steadfast, joyous pursuit of truth.

Ray McManus for his brilliant artistic vision and representation of *The Archaeology of Peace*. Formerly residing in Manchester, England, McManus now lives in Ireland. An Irish artist, McManus is the originator of the artistic technique called the squiggle, reminiscent of the Celtic knot. McManus transcends the traditional decorative application of the Celtic knot using his interwoven knots as abstract expressions of Jim's themes in this spiraling vortex drawing our focus deeply down into the core. Thank you from my very soul—the English term *thank you* is a paltry expression compared to the profundity of your elegant squiggles.

Rajesh Maurya for his gorgeous cover design. A talented graphic artist and media expert in New Delhi, India, Rajesh offered his beautiful inspiration in time to rescue a floundering project. Thank you so much for all your talented effort on this project! You are the catalyst to the finish!

Satya Das, good friend and respected colleague, AVP for content production at Kaplan in New Delhi, India, thank you so much for caring about our book! Thank you for your generous action; you reignited this project with your compassionate and thoughtful offering of help and support. In the spirit of freedom and in peace, I thank you, dearest friend.

Richard Magee, Jim's enduring friend and lively sparring partner for all things abstract and debatable, thank you for your wise insight into the holistic nature of freedom.

Marypat Green, for her gorgeous golden eagle logo: thank you for the beautiful design gracing all three of Jim's books!

Jonathon Jacob O'Brien, our son, our life's inspiration. For you, we strove to be and share our best selves. In you, we see the future; we feel the 'why' of our existence.

1
PHILOSOPHY

✤ ✤ ✤

The multi-faceted world of philosophical expression contains no gem more alluring than the archaeology of presuppositions, assumptions, and leading principles. We, as critical thinkers, want to know the framework from which our thoughts issue. The concrete experience we live is pregnant with meanings and undisclosed possibilities for action. The awareness of the full phenomena of consciousness and its relation to its intellectual grounds is the chief end of philosophical reflection. Everything that is in some way present to the mind can be critically integrated in accordance with the dictates of the mind.

Philosophy needs to raise questions that can lead to fruitful insight into the meaning of life and the utility of various actions. Since thought is all about action, rational discourse seeks its limits in ultimate values and experiential harmony. In short, the natural mind seeks self-fulfillment and a congenial concordance with all life.

Thought must address itself to action for action is the point upon which commitments are made. Action structures experience by relating phenomena in a definite manner. The rational mind could create endless combinations of various events and particulars if certain patterns did not dominate consciousness with their concrete consistency and completeness. This definite and fulfilled world is the region of concrete action where one thing influences another in an irrevocable manner. The consciousness of nature is the consciousness of things and events acting on one another.

We not only observe the action of the things of the world, but we reflectively follow the impulses of our actions. Our thoughts are structured by their capacity to satisfy the conditions of action. A successful thought is an idea that benefits action by providing significance and cognitive order for the life of the mind. For example, my thought about trees, expresses a set of satisfying values (feelings) about tree/worlds which enable me to enter into a definite relationship with trees and do definite things with trees.

Another way of looking at it is to imagine that all the things that a mind observes acting on one another converge, in reflection, on a point that is itself the most satisfying condition for individual human action. Thus, human action is an ultimate structure for human reflection. Thought and action belong together.

There are many serious, long-standing problems in human life. Yet, none are more destructive than war. War is not only an ugly fact of human history but an event that I find quite unjustifiable. The following argument should help explain my anti-war assertion and provide insight for further exploration of human culture.

2
WAR AND JUSTIFICATION
✤ ✤ ✤

War is almost never ethically justifiable. War is an organized effort of institutions to subjugate or kill the members of rival institutions. Most commonly the institutions are the military forces of nations. The essential military actions of war kill and enslave human beings, and often on a relatively large scale. Killing someone is a way of terminating that person's capacity to feel, think, and act. The manifestations of feeling, thinking, and acting are the expressions of a person's existence, the freedom to create possibilities and act on them. Thus, killing shares an affinity with enslavement in that both destroy, completely or partially, the vital freedom of human beings. Killing could be described as the final assault on freedom, the ultimate termination of another's possibilities to feel, think and act.

Why is destroying another's freedom immoral? Whatever good we may desire can only come from feeling, thinking and acting. In other words, to acquire a good (something of value) we must be able to feel its value, signify its meaning and pursue its possession. Thus, to obtain any good at all, we must exist and in such a manner that we can feel, think and act to a degree necessary to obtain our desired goods. If a military force prevents a Buddhist monk from meditating at a wall, the good monk has had a dearly beloved set of possibilities taken from him. That is, the possibilities of feeling and thinking as well as non-thinking with the Buddha have been eliminated by alien force. Of course, the monk can pursue new possibilities, meditate secretly, or immolate himself in symbolic rejection of the world, but the fact remains that a greatly valued good has been taken from him. And it is like this with all goods from the taste of chocolate ice cream to the embrace of our fondest lover. The necessary conditions for having any good at all are existence and the freedom to feel, think, and act in pursuit of the good.

The individual human pursuit of the good is in fierce and irrevocable competition with the aims at destroying existence and its freedom to feel, think, and act. Thus, the pursuit of goods, which is necessarily grounded in human freedom, is attacked by the use of military force. Now, since the very capacity to pursue good is attacked by warfare, it is logically impossible that warfare can be an expression of an ethical will. For what aims to prevent good cannot logically be an expression of good.

Of course, if we have a political power that is sure of its survival and that its liberties will be only temporarily suspended, it may decide to solve a problem by military force. However, such a power is still violating the principle of freedom. To pursue your own freedom while simultaneously trying to destroy another's freedom is not an expression of freedom, but rather of power. For to express freedom, as a principle, is to affirm the state of affairs that represents liberty as a desirable condition for all mankind. As the great Kant said, we universalize our maxims when we think logically about morals. To prevent another from pursuing its goods or the good while pursuing our own ideal is logically incompatible with the principles of moral action. We cannot logically affirm the pursuit of the good while actively trying to terminate the pursuit of the good.

The aim of warfare is to kill and subjugate an enemy people. This clearly cannot be ethically justified. By 'ethically justified', I mean that such activities cannot be judged moral by acts of reasoning. On the contrary, the dictates of reason condemn war as fundamentally immoral.

Are there any cases when war could be ethically justifiable? Only cases when war is the only way in which our survival and vital freedom can be preserved. For example, if a military force landed on your nation's shores with the express intent of conquest, then no doubt it would be justified to defend your land and people with violent reciprocation. However, even in such a case, the ideal would be to try a nonviolent means of settling the conflict. War is only justified as a last resort.

The justifying concept of self-preservation is sometimes extended to the protection of 'friends'. If a political ally or even a friendly neighbor is attacked by a military force, it is possible to justifiably come to the aid of our friend. I say possible, because such protective military involvement can only be justified if the protective action is a clear expression of the principle of liberty or moral right. Or some principle that affirms a peoples' right to self-preservation and liberty. Giving military aid to other nations presupposes a principle of liberty or it is not morally justified. The protecting nation must affirm the right and value of liberty for all nations and act in accordance with this principle. To attack the enemies of some of our friends and to turn away blindly from tyranny elsewhere in the world does not indicate acting from ethical principles of liberty. Indeed, unless there is a consistent support for every nation that is tyrannized and for every society that is tyrannized by its own nation, then there is no rational grounds for claiming to be acting morally.

3
THE ARGUMENT
✤ ✤ ✤

My anti-war argument may benefit from a little intellectual archaeology? The argument asserts that warfare is self-contradictory for it destroys the capacity to freely pursue good, thus undermining its claims to be acting for the good. Destroy freedom and you destroy the capacity for both good and evil. Thus, to combat 'evil' by destroying the freedom of agents to act for good or evil is itself immoral and irrational. Irrational because it destroys the very end it posits and pursues.

An immediate critical response to this anti-war argument is to claim that armies only seek their own particular good, and respect only their own freedom. There is no acceptance and affirmation of a general freedom to pursue desired ends. The enemy's freedom is to be crushed. The good is simply my side's goals.

However, it is not clear that some people have an innate right to life and liberty and others do not! On the contrary, freedom defined as the creative power to think, feel and act is an essential character of a human being. And any judgment that denies the right to liberty for some people treats those excluded as something less valued than a human being. Our natural right to liberty is grounded in an ideal that humans are essentially free. That is, a human being is an animal with the capacity to conceive and pursue its own ends.

The anti-war argument claims that any attempt at moral justification that denies the innate right to freedom for some people is logically inconsistent and dehumanizing. But, the pro-war individual may not arbitrarily claim the right to freedom for his group alone. More often, the war advocate will simply claim the 'right' to pursue his ends. Here, the 'right' is simply the exercise of power. 'Freedom' is only the freedom to act for his/her group and not a considered possibility for any other group. Thus, it is not the essential freedom that defines us as a human being, but the power to act on certain private interests that express as the warmonger's position.

Pursuing your own ends with no recognition of a right for the others to pursue their ends reduces freedom to power. To act in such a way as to reflect the value of freedom is to affirm not only your own liberty but also the freedom of the others who exist in your world. It is everybody's freedom that I affirm when I select the value of freedom as my way of relating to the world.

On the other hand, it is only my own 'freedom' that I affirm when I select the value of power as my way of solving a problem.

The anti-war argument advocates freedom. As free, rational beings, we ought not desire conquest. We want the 'other' to be free. The world is a coming and going of free beings in search of reciprocal harmony. By sharp contrast, the warmonger wants an enemy to defeat, a victory to claim and a position of dominance; in short, the warmonger is all about power. Thus, claims of freedom are at their base simply power plays for the lovers of violence.

When freedom is reduced to power (the usual political arrangement amongst nations) the actual controlling maxim in life is 'might makes right'!

'Might makes right' means that there are no innate rights, no grounds for justification, no rationality in governing life, no self-justifying impulses, and no harmony with the natural and social universes. Taken at its word, 'might makes right' reduces the relationship to society to one of irrational and pitiless thirsting for dominance, while the relationship to the natural world becomes one of unbridled exploitation.

Our archaeological dig has unearthed a few assumptions that need exploration. My anti-war argument rests on the idea of freedom. Thus, the nature of freedom needs to be probed. And since we want a broad and clear-eyed probing I will do some phenomenologically. The other assumptions I want to explore concern the generality of concepts necessary for rational justification. We need to speak of the general truths of existence in order to impart a guiding structure and consistency for our values and deeds.

4
FREEDOM
✤ ✤ ✤

Events! An event is the creative emergence of certain possibilities. The emergent possibilities express creative power. It is only by the free manifestation of original possibilities that experience comes to be. The event is a relationship constituted by a world and a consciousness. There is no knowable world without a consciousness and there is no consciousness that is not a consciousness of something. At bottom, there exists a given.

The objects we perceive in the world are, at bottom, relationships between a consciousness and a world. A 'tree' is not a physical object independent of a mind, but a particular relationship constituted by a creative mind. The possibilities that actualize as a 'tree' are possibilities for definite relationship.

In the emergence of an event there are two irreducibly unique centers or agencies. One of the unique agents is the creative consciousness that constitutes the experience of the event. The other irreducible phenomenon is the object in the field of experience that consciousness focuses on. If I am observing a 'tree', then the 'tree' is the center from which an environment flows out. The environment exists as objects belonging to the interdependent character of the 'tree'. But, the 'tree' is the center from which things develop. And, like the human mind, it is an irreducibly unique agent. As experience changes, the focus of consciousness shifts and new unique agents express themselves in the world.

Creativity brings about self-awareness and our consciousness of a world. Creativity environs a world for those unique agents that are the focus of our consciousness. Thus, there are many creative sources expressing unique possibilities for being in the world. We are closer to nature and each other than we realize. For there is an affinity between the various sources of creativity. We can intellectually identify with the creative processes of other life forms. Perhaps, in creative affinities dwells the source of true knowledge.

Freedom is a structure of the universe. And individual events are expressions of free, creative powers. I express my freedom by relating to my environment in a unique way. From a field of possibilities I spontaneously and reflectively shape myself by the distinctive way I relate to my environment.

Freedom is the creative capacity to participate in the shaping of a universe. Human freedom is the unique way each of us shapes his/her environed self. We bring out the possibilities inherent in our freedom in order to liberate or 'perfect' ourselves. The major modes that freedom works through are spontaneity and reflection. Spontaneity includes the instinctual and emotional responses we make in relating to a given world. It brings out our natural desires and joys in the intensity of their full immediacy. We participate as a stream of diverse perceptions and affections in spontaneous freedom's shaping of a particular world.

Reflective freedom is simply freedom of thought. However, freedom of thought is not a purely abstract (formal) activity, but a comprehensive thinking whose function is no less than the total integration of human experience. The vast and varied manifold of pre-reflective experience challenges the philosophical intellect to accurately distinguish and synthesize its structure and meaning.

The healthy functioning of spontaneous and reflective freedom gives us a richly varied experience and lucid patterns of conduct. The world of the free mind is broad, flexible, unified, and elegantly diversified. The world of the un-free mind is characterized by narrowness, rigidity, deep conceptual incongruence, logical contradiction, and conventionality.

A free mind is creative process that is nourished by a flow of impressions, feeling, and percepts freed up by an act of self-acceptance and openness. A free, reflective mind is a creative process that is cultivated by a constant curiosity, critical probing, and the architectonic structuring of events. The free thinker creates harmony and order in the region where the 'non-thinker' is insecure and troubled out of intellectual blindness and superficial, unjustified assumptions. On the other hand, the free thinker creates anxiety and conflict by critically questioning life and society, which the 'non-thinker' conforms to without a serious doubt. The thinker's harmony is at the foundations, structures, and ends of life. To be a thinker is to create order by ceaseless self-reflection. The price of such a 'life/choice' is the uncertainty and anxiety of putting everything in question as the reflective process explores and develops. The creative philosopher is 'gamboling' that independent discovery and intellectual harmony will offset the pain of being an independent mind.

5

TRUTH
✤ ✤ ✤

The great philosopher, Edmund Husserl, contemplated the thought of Descartes: "I, the solitary individual, owe much to other persons, but what they offer to me as truth, at first, is only something they claim. To accept it I must justify it by a perfect insight of my own."

The intellectual fruits of the grand meditation were the concise ideas imbued within the maxim above. Descartes' maxims have an intuitive elegance, simplicity, and rightness about them. Husserl's contemplation of Descartes' thought is fittingly lucid, concise, and beautiful. Husserl's insight goes deep to the nature of knowledge, itself. What makes something 'true'? Why accept an idea as true, or even worthy? The philosopher writes, "Truth, at first, is only something they claim." Knowledge does not come from the uncritical acceptance of others' views. It does not come from others at all.

Knowledge comes from within ourselves, as reflective individuals. Husserl expressed it this way: "To accept it I must justify it by a perfect insight of my own." The American philosopher, Sherman Stanage, interprets Husserl's thought as, "Knowledge emerges from the reaching out for the 'perfect'." Husserl's insight presupposes the freedom of the human mind. It is we, each as a distinct individual, who constitute knowledge with the creative power of particular acts of reason!

Perfection births truth. Yet, it is a limited perfection, for truth is open to many insights. One perfection may even be such that it shows the falseness of perfection. Both thoughts express authentic intellectual perfection, but their respective perfections refer to slightly different worlds.

A given truth admits of multiple perfections. One perfection may show the falsity of another perfection by pointing to what was not captured by the other truth. A critical perfection may capture the larger framework, in which the criticized perfection is situated, thus, granting its truth within its region of expression while showing its lack in the greater universe of expression.

A truth is not a closed and final affair. It is open to revision and reformation. The concrete sequence of events that constitutes our experiences seems beyond human intelligence's capacity to comprehend fully. With perfect insight we differentiate a 'piece' of the universe, but time and further reflection show us false. Perfection is perfection. We leave it untouched with the 'advance' of our thoughts. Yet, single perfections do not exhaust the possibilities of truth.

The concepts by which we constitute a world are strung together in a grand web. Each distinct concept is limited in its individuality for its 'uniqueness is the way it stands out from a shared conceptual foundation. In short, our concepts are generic. And our intellectual universe is an 'interdependent' whole.

Experience as the grounds for all our thoughts and concepts may be an inexhaustible mine of infinite wealth. Thus, Absolute truth is an illusion and truth is an exploration marked by a series of limited perfections.

A 'perfect/insight' suggests a relationship so fine that it is beyond the intellect's need for any alteration or refinement. The relationship is one between a consciousness and its object. As I understand this epistemological relationship it is an act of love. This is so because the object of thought is 'held' in loving contemplation by the meditative mind.

The perfection is the harmony of the intellect and its object. The interaction between the mind and its contemplated object attains a unity where all perturbations and conflict have been overcome in an act of perfect/insight. Only an all-abiding peace remains. Of course, the finite curiosity and fluidness of experience intervenes undermining our temporary peace and perfection. The life of the mind and its universe are ceaselessly in process.

6
REASON
✤ ✤ ✤

Rational thought describes and explains our phenomenal world. In its purest form, thought is an effort to coherently describe everything that in some way comes into the mind. Yet, all thought, even the purest philosophy, expresses some interest in articulation of its concepts.

Philosopher Jurgen Habermas has shown that the interests are primarily cognitive and come in two main forms: 1) thought that seeks to control the environment that the thinking being exists in. The 'cognitive/interest', which shapes the direction thought will take is 'power over things' (prediction and control). We call this 'instrumental reasoning'. And it is the domain of physical science; 2) thought that seeks to exist in harmony with its environment and to intellectually fuse with its object. Here, the 'cognitive/interest' is liberation, or the perfection of the self through the cultivation of free powers. The domain is creative philosophy and all disciplines and activities that contribute to its grand project. I call this thought 'comprehensive reasoning'.

Instrumental reasoning is a way of logically pursuing blind ends. It is concerned with the means to achieve something, and not with the value or nature of the end. In contrast, comprehensive reflection focuses on the ends, the ultimate value, and nature of things, bringing means into play only as applications of well-grounded theoretical aims and ideas. The comprehensive mind lets nature be so as to speak to us as it is, and not only as we wish it to. The instrumental mind asks no questions and pays no heed to nature, itself. It simply abstracts what will enable it to secure a conceptual and practical control over things.

The general interests that are closest to the actual processes of reflection are self-perfection and its pre-condition of freedom. Thought articulates an intelligent/order out of experience. The intelligent/order, when fully determined, shows the human mind its own image and its possibilities for being in a world that is free of our designs and controls. Thus, the world is not an object of our utility, but rather an essential component of a seminal relationship with our most elemental self.

In seeking to perfect ourselves, we give liberty to our curiosity and authority to our critical spirit. We can find ourselves only in also finding the world we exist with. To know this world intimately we need to see it beyond our designs of utility. We need to see it 'perfectly' as it exists with us in loving intellectual union.

Reason is often pitted against power in cultural life. We want events to be rationally grounded for it constitutes a general structure that is potentially congenial for all involved. Rather than force her conformity and private interest, we, if rational, opt for reasoned judgment in all affairs. Freedom is the pre-condition for rational discourse and communication rationally directed creates an intellectual climate of liberty and social tolerance.

In social life, reason ought to strongly prevail over force and fashion. And the general intellectual world ought to give the cognitive/interest of liberation top seeing. For the aim of liberation is much greater than the aim of control over things. Indeed, control over nature can only be logically justified by a thinking that originates in the quest for liberation and perfection.

7

STRANGENESS

✣ ✣ ✣

I am going to explore the concept of 'strangeness'. The exploration will only be a preliminary probing of the region most immediately of interest to me. Thus, my intention is to structure my probing around the social consequences of the way persons interpret the meaning of 'strangeness'.

The familiar act of deliberately encountering the uncertain, unknown and unforeseen, expresses courage and intellectual curiosity. The concept of 'strangeness' invites us to engage in a less than secure and predictable world. We may reject the 'invitation', and thus lose the possible joys and benefits of exploration and creation. However, there is no escape from strangeness in some form.

The world is a highly differentiated unity. We are basically provincial beings bound to familiar landmarks and practical vision. Therefore, much of the differentiated cosmos appears unfamiliar, at times, even dangerous to we domestic souls. Our language is practical and prosaic. Yet, metaphor lurks at the horizon and novel possibilities of thought weep to the threshold of consciousness creating disquiet and anxiety in our prosaic minds. Of course, we can live in a vast, inflexible rut and fight off all impulses to novelty. Yet, something will always appear less stable and predictable than something else, and inconsistencies of thought and unforeseen social experiences will visit us.

'Strangeness' is part of our awareness of novelty. For something to appear 'Strange' is an opportunity for excitement, learning, and discovery. Of course, it has its dangers. Even the most powerful animals (tigers) are very nervous and cautious around human nets placed across their territories. Evolution has 'taught' them to be wary and careful. Humans should also be cautious with unknown things and circumstances. However, evolution and tigers aside, humans tend strongly to over caution, or outright timidity before the uncertain and the unknown. Forging a unique self requires a healthy acceptance of novelty and exploration in order to discover and cultivate our best potentials. To be the distinct person each of us is naturally demands risking novel experiences and new territories to dwell in. Indeed, personal exploration is a rational aim of self-perfection.

The fear of unknown and strange phenomena can have devastating social consequences. For example, the child who looks a little different or acts in peculiar ways can become a target of collective hostility. A feared object to be shunned and isolated from the 'normal' fellows is the sad outcome of individuals whose differences are interpreted as undesirable and socially threatening. Now, I am not referring to cases where an individual is clearly violent and being kept away from society for reasons of safety. Rather, we are dealing with normal cases of social violence toward individuals who in one way or another do not meet the social norms. Some of these outcasts are the wrong color or size, others cannot learn academics, and some are extremely talented (Socrates), while still others just don't pursue the common goals (money).

Ostracizing individuals because they do not fit the mold, so to speak, is a form of mob mentality. It says, "You, 'different one', are not wanted—you are just not one-of-us." The 'one-of-us' concept substitutes as an identity for the independent character that would develop, as a distinct personality, if freedom of thought and action were encouraged (or at least tolerated). Now, in my experience, nearly all social groups tend toward this arbitrary isolating of individuals. In a country with a tradition for individualism and self-reliance you might expect otherwise? Thoreau and Emerson, the great non-conformists of American thought, have not for the most part been heeded. Rather, it is corporate uniformity and an uncritical consensus on the rightness of pursuing wealth that dominates contemporary culture.

The problem is complex. Included in the problem is our concept of 'Strangeness'. The inability to handle strange persons and circumstances in a rational manner for a great many normal persons contributes mightily to social intolerance, tyranny, and violence. Perhaps the 'strangeness' that is most difficult to live with is that buried deep within our breast.

8
PEACE
✤ ✤ ✤

Elementary conceptions are concealed in the folds of experience making excavation difficult for even deeply philosophic minds. Once in the garden on a warm, sunny day, I stared into the blue petals of a wildflower. All boundaries dissolved, only blueness remaining in an infinite extension.

Experiencing just a vast blueness suggests a method of seeing things, more or less alone. The phenomenon of blueness was seen in isolation from its universe. The possibility of being blue was captured as an immediate experience of blueness, all bud itself. What would 'strangeness' be like seen in a similar way? The pure presence of 'Strangeness' will be much different consciousness than the quality of blueness. 'Strangeness' is not a sensation but an irregularity in a pattern, and an unfamiliarity with this oddity. Events that are perceived as having a different sequence and structure than similar, but more common, events do not conform to the expected scenario for such occurrences. The possible conditions for insecurity, fear, and eventually hostility are present in the phenomenological disclosure of 'Strangeness'. Yet, so is the possibility of adventure, exploration, and eventually discovery.

Peace! For us to experience peace in any fairly enduring way requires that the possible conditions enveloping the phenomena of 'strangeness' be ones of adventure and discovery. Yet, this clearly is not enough. Peace is a kind of harmony where all agents live in a way that is deeply satisfying for both the community and each of the individuals composing the whole. Thus, in the universe of peace there are many values and ways. Yet, this diversity of life only contributes to the solidarity and satisfaction of the community.

The ideal of peace is an alpine affair with steep climbs and possible storms. There is no contradiction between an individual seeking personal satisfaction and the ideal goals of the community to which the striving individual belongs. Every one of us, no matter what group we dwell in, is an innately distinct individual. Freedom is a universal value. We all ought to do it our own way. Conflict is inevitable, but not necessarily destructive. Like 'Strangeness' it is only an occasion for various possibilities of thought and action.

The ideal is simple. A community can morally prohibit individuals only from acts that are harmful to the freedom of others. The most common violations are murder, enslavement, torture, coercion, and social alienation for being in some sense 'out of step'. Beyond prohibiting and discouraging these violatives the community has no justifiable moral authority. If an individual wants to be lazy, weird, and even 'undesirable' it is up to him or her. It is not a matter of law or social control. To make it a legal matter is to do violence to the nature of peace. For peace demands that each individual treat every other individual as a free, autonomous agent. That is a fundamental condition for rational, harmonious living in a community.

A community needs cooperation and practical participation in its affairs to succeed. When individuals do not share the load in a community, it is not a problem of law or social sanctions. Individuals must be free to 'join in' or 'not join in'. It needs to be a voluntary way. The solution to the problem of the lack of constructive participation is ideally educational. The community must motivate by bringing about a realization in the minds of its members of the significance and rationality of cooperative living. And remember, rational knowledge is always a personal intuition of perfection or it is not knowledge at all. Knowledge presupposes freedom of thought.

Person's tasks constituting a rational community are very difficult to understand. It cannot morally force, coerce, seduce, or 'program' its members into conformity with its social design. On the contrary, the 'community' must do all that it can to prevent its members from committing such violatives against one another. Yet, it needs to mobilize collective power and action sufficient to meet its ends.

9
UNIQUENESS
✤ ✤ ✤

Every single person is unique. Our problem is in accepting that we are each a clearly distinct, irreducibly unique being that is integrated with the whole universe. We 'insist' on seeing ourselves as normal, a variation on a standard mold. And we strive to attain the state of affairs that will bring status, power, security and 'belongingness' to a hard, fine end for us. The ideal proves ever-elusive and we vainly chase our tails in the circle of social charades.

We cannot find ourselves in the image and form others have create for us. We cannot find ourselves in the 'standard' for we are at bottom truly rare.

I want to look just as I am, give or take a few pounds. My face is as it is. My body can be trained to a fine edge in accordance with my natural frame. This is part of my way of trying to accept myself. I am not concerned with the fashions, 'classical forms,' and other public models that society tantalizes us with. I do not need to compete for a place in schemes designed by other people's fancies! I only need to accept and perfect myself.

Thus, I am not a social engineer in any strict sense of the meaning of that concept. We cannot make another 'see' or 'understand' or 'authentically be'. I don't know enough to precisely predict what would happen from a 'given' set of social conditions implemented to transform a given society. I do know that freedom is essential. So, I only suggest better ways of dealing with conditions and problems.

We, as distinct selves, are streams within the universe. We, as human beings, are creative participants in a vast network of relationships that constitute the web of events comprising the universe. Thus, I, an irreducibly unique agent, can recommend 'uniqueness' and 'freedom' for all other free beings in the universe we share. I can also discern the commonalities we free agents share in existing together in the world. Last, I can hope for a better 'state of affairs' for all of us. And I can write about it. This is my way of being a rational benefit to my society!

Let us consider fashioning a culture that is congenial with the values of freedom, rationality, uniqueness, and peace.

Our phenomenological analysis has given us a coherent description/classification of experience, reason, existence, and community.

This analysis can serve as the grounds for certain keystone values of human life for essential values express generally desirable ends, which often are only 'outcomes' of innate processes and structures of life. We enjoy and take deep pleasure in our freedom because we are free beings existing in a world of free beings. Essentially desirable ends are functions of the satisfaction and meaning of being, itself.

The prime values that can be lucidly inferred from our phenomenological reasonings are Universal Freedom, rationality, the celebration of uniqueness, and peace. These values when manifest truly can occasion the germination of the 'perfect' human society. A community of free beings living cooperatively in free and harmonious interaction with each other and their environment.

The health of a culture can be estimated by determining the extent to which the given culture distances itself from the prime values of Universal Freedom, Rationality, The Celebration of Uniqueness, and Peace. The greater the distancing the more cruel and unhealthy the society. Since a culture is only the total communicative interaction of its individuals, social problems are a matter of concern for everyone. The whole does not exist without the constituting power of its members. The responsibility of the individual is eminent in the interdependent network of lives we call a culture. So, the prime values need to pervade the whole culture in order to be effective in transforming culture.

The transformation of culture in accordance with our keystone values is necessary for the happiness and well being of the human species. Indeed, the very preservation of human society may depend upon our attainment of such values. Our major institutions need to be transformed according to the rational dictates of the keystone values. The task is immense, utopic, and visionary. However, a modest 'beginning' could start off by isolating certain outstanding problems. These problems would first be analyzed in relation to our value scheme and then relevant transformational scenarios could be drawn up. In this spirit, I will make some critical probings into contemporary politics and culture.

10
GOVERNMENT
✣ ✣ ✣

The best government is the government that clearly supports its culture's will to affirm and celebrate the keystone values of Universal Freedom, Rationality, The Celebration of Uniqueness, and Peace. Obviously, no present world power is anywhere near this ideal. Measuring contemporary America against this value scale and expecting positive results is like asking an American bull terrier to explain the complete science and philosophy of Albert Einstein. In spite of this, it should prove salutary to probe into some ideas about modern government.

The social thinker, Thomas Jefferson, claimed that the government that governs least is the best government. At a higher philosophical level, Emerson finds truth in ordinary life with government being largely a hypocritical, intervening evil. Still wider and higher in the thought universe is CS Peirce, who deviates from the uncritical praise of American liberty. This American philosopher asserts that the capitalist system of late 19th century America is a will to selfishness and unreflective existence. Peirce advocates a doctrine of universal sympathy where all thinking beings take care and responsibility for one another.

Why would a government that governs little be thought to be superior as a government?

To govern is to direct or control lives and communities. And an essential value of existence is the freedom to exist in a unique manner. Government, to some extent, interferes with that personal quest to exist as we desire. It also takes away from the pride and confidence of our self-reliance to be directed by a paternal, political authority. Jefferson and Emerson (and Peirce for that matter) value freedom highly. These thinkers represent and reflect much of the best in American culture. Thus, it is not surprising that political authority and government, in general, are observed with suspicion and evaluated critically. That is all as it should rationally be. However, there are many problems with the ideas of a non-interfering government!

A non-interfering government, even a Taoist system, is still a form of government. And the citizens of the government construct and sustain modes of relating and life styles that complement their form of government. Thus, it is imperative to explore the relationship between individuals and society. In particular, what is the best relationship between an individual and his/her community?

The 'individual' is a concrete actuality, while 'society' is a derived abstraction. The abstract concept of 'society' issues out from the creative mind of a concrete individual. The foundation for our abstract concepts is a concrete, individualized consciousness. A society cannot exist independent of the individual minds that constitute it. Individuals do not by nature live in isolation for we form our selves in interaction with others. There is always an influential human environment enveloping our personal selves. Yet, a government is only that part of a society that directs its legitimate, political activities. And a society is just that part of a human environment that corresponds to a field of circumscribed interests and activities. In the interaction of concrete individuals certain relatively constant relations form a collective unity. When the collective unity consists of sufficient diversity of interest and action to reflect a practical way of life, we call it a society. Societies are created by individuals and represent only aspects of our interdependent existence.

Some philosophers prefer to give emphasis to the whole rather than the part. However, societies, and even more so governments, are not representative of the whole. The 'whole' is the sum total of all individual interactions, or a pre-existent mind/structure for all discourse, or the network of concrete agents that constitute a world, or perhaps a cosmic oneness. The 'whole' is always much greater than the complexity possible in the concept of a 'society'.

A concrete individual belongs to reality. Reality, if you want, is the 'whole'. And 'society', like 'individual', is a concept expressing a structure of Reality. Society is a derived structure constituted by creative individuals from a field of possible interactions for a bounded group. Thus, an 'individual' takes precedence over a 'society' in regard to the nature of things.

The subordination of the 'individual' to 'society' is irrational for a society's only meaning comes from making life better for individuals. And individuals do not rationally serve society except as it enhances their individuality and well being. A creator cannot become a slave to his/her creation, or the creation, which originally expressed unique value and deep aspiration, turns against its designs to devour vitality, understanding, and freedom. The creative agent is no longer creative when obligated to servitude before the authority of the institution which the creator in the beginning designed for his/her satisfaction. So, strictly speaking, an individual cannot logically serve the state for that would contradict the original state of mind that feels, constitutes, and invents. In short, we create something that destroys our creative processing.

Fascist governments assert the dominance of the state over the individual. However, it is not only 'Nazis' that are socially vulgar and irrational. American president, J.F. Kennedy proudly challenged American citizens to, "Ask not what your country can do for you, but rather what you can do for your country." This confused and badly stated maxim may conceal a thread of truth. The flowering of selfhood is often attained by commitments to the well-being of others. Our individuality blooms by acting to enhance and celebrate the uniqueness and liberty of all beings. Thus, to best serve our personal liberty and selfhood we need to respect and affirm the rights of others. This fine ethical attitude can become a principle for designing and directing communal activity. Even, in some cases, a legitimate duty to society. However, such legitimate duties and admirable servicing of others does not show a dominance of society over the individual, but rather that a way of cultivating individuality is through expressing respect and concern for other individuals. Thus, extending the range of individuals to be respected. The wider our extension of respect, the better for us. To love, not only our family, but all persons, is noble. Better yet is the love of all organic life, and still better to love all being. The greater the range of application for genuine sympathy and respect, the greater our gain in status as free persons. We grow, as persons, by relating with others in a free, affirming manner, for our autonomy expresses our essential involvement with things. I freely enjoy my trek in the wild verdant forest for my body/mind is intimately related to the tree/environment, and my free, spontaneous participation in the forest life expresses this intimate harmony.

In social life, as well as in nature, we are essentially involved as creative agents woven into a social web. However, the social community is less elemental than the purely natural environment and more subject to confusion and destruction.

The non-interfacing government would be the sufficient solution if there were not other social agencies than governments that violate human freedom. However, much of the suppression of freedom in a culture is occasioned by non-governmental institutions. The authoritarian disposition of parents, schools, and churches combined with the slick propaganda of the market place and media marshal a formative assault on individual autonomy. While there are many liberties in the pursuit of amusements and many ways to pursue material gain in our society, the capacity for critical reflection remains depressed. Conformity to a materialist model stressing obedience to authority, wealth, industry, selfishness, and insatiable consumption is rigorous, allowing for little free dissent. Worse yet, the very means to bring about constructive dissent and creative transformation is undermined in contemporary culture. We do not accept a full, healthy rationality. The nature, value, and ultimate ends of our problems and the possible solutions are not seriously reflected upon. Our 'rationality' is simply the application of techniques to attain ends, which are blind to us. Lacking critical rationality and a serious philosophy we tend to flounder about in a sea of cultural waves generated by market movements, fashion, politics, and custom.

Since there are so many institutions that do violence to human freedom, it is necessary to intervene in cultural life on behalf of the individual. We are justified in seeking certain social controls that will protect and promote individual rights. The government cannot be completely powerless if we expect it to play a role in preserving the freedom of individuals.

It is the individual that is primary and the source of actual freedom. Society and government are not justified in subjugating the individuals who constitute its body. The body politic must be the free creation of autonomous individuals. On the other hand, particular individuals and institutions can act to exploit and enslave the 'free' persons in their environment. Strictly speaking, a social institution is not justified in directing the lives of its individual citizens for the institutions exist only to serve free, rational agents. But then, how can a community take steps to constrain exploitation, violence, and enslavement? Laws and customs that constrain individuals from violencing one another are not constraints of freedom seen as a whole process. The rules only constrain possible acts that would destroy the reciprocity of individual freedoms and the principle of freedom in general. In other words, rational 'laws' prohibiting the treating of individuals as means to ends, while implying that all individuals are ends, free agents. The constraint of the custom and law actually enhances and increases the universe of free activity. The particular prohibition makes possible the free interaction of persons in their environments. And the limits formed by the rules are attacks on illegitimate authority, power, and chaos.

Thus, laws and social controls that enhance rather than negate the process of freedom are rational and legitimate. Laws that violate the process of freedom are irrational and socially illegitimate. Hence, there exists grounds for the rational interference of society in the affairs of individual persons.

Sometimes it is not government, itself, that is most coercive. The 'private sector' or corporate economic segment of society is far more violent toward freedom than the government, proper. Dedicated to wielding 'persons' into a uniform 'machine' for making profits, indifferent to those outside its range of utility, and hostile to anything perceived as getting in their way, the contemporary corporate universe creates great social problems. The horror of the government's war machine and the programmed poverty of the welfare state are inseparable from the commanding influence of economic leaders. As is the mindless, anti-rational education that is force-fed to American youth, and so on. We could go through all the major institutions of American life listing the destructive influences of the 'private sector'.

Who should govern? The question logically leads to considerations of the conditions for having satisfying communal relations. What is the desideratum for people governing being governed? Dostoyevsky's grand inquisitor seeks to purge humans from the terrible condition of freedom. As this most unusual tyrant sees it, humans fear and hate their own capacity for self-awareness, choice, critique, and personal transformation. Thus the inquisitor acts out of grand 'humane' motives by enslaving and torching the poor souls who suffer under freedom. He alleviates our inescapable pain by removing us from our essence (freedom), from which we desperately flee.

The grand inquisitor is unique amongst tyrants. The logic of an ordinary tyrant is strictly functional. What is 'rational' is whatever functions efficiently in achieving a goal. The functional rationality of a tyrant is of no use in understanding the nature of the action the tyrant is engaged in. Technique only produces results and not insight into what the 'results' are all about. For example, the Nazi leader, Adolph Eichmann, regarded his actions as rational simply because he perceived his violence as an efficient means to solve a problem. However, things are different for that great fictional tyrant, the grand inquisitor. He seeks a philosophical justification for his violence.

Great violence is not 'rational' because it is effectively organized. The grand tyrant is not acting because he was ordered to, nor justifying himself by appeal to authority. No, he reflects on the human condition and acts in accordance with the results of his meditations. Freedom is the source of human misery and its excision the 'life cure'. If this maxim were rational it would be a case of full, comprehensive rationality, and not simply functional (instrumental) rationality. Of course, it is not rational to think that freedom is essentially evil for it is only through freedom that we can experience anything good or evil. If freedom, broadly conceived, goes, then everything goes. Yet, Dostoyevsky's character is irrational in the high country of the mind and that makes him rather unique amongst the major tyrants.

So, the guiding principle that freedom is a horror to be escaped from is not justifiable, for if freedom exists, everything else, good and bad, necessarily opens upon freedom's creative functioning. However, one could abstractly choose 'nothing' rather than freedom. If all follows from freedom's constitution of a world, then a negation of freedom would embrace a psychic void, a 'nothingness'. Is it rational to prefer 'nothingness' to the pain and adventure of a free life? The grand inquisitor may think so, but only at the price of denying all spontaneous 'impulses' to know, care, appreciate, interact with, and, in general, relate to the universe. In short, the attempt to choose 'nothingness' is an attempt to do the impossible, to negate experience, itself.

The grand inquisitor does not represent the ordinary tyrant. The 'will to power' over others, functional rationality and an authoritarian, cultural setting are all that are normally required for the appearance of a tyrant. In contemporary Western society, a tyrant cannot rule as a tyrant, but rather must disguise his cruel thirst under a veil of jingoism and righteousness. The 'tyrant' must be thought to be a legitimate representative of the citizens. So the best way to be governed cannot be tyrannical in the eyes of the contemporary person. We can cancel out the overt tyrant as a present-day model for good government.

The conditions for selecting who ought to govern include the determining of what is the best way to govern and be governed. With overt tyranny ruled out, we can turn our analysis to representative government. The general problem for freedom in a representative government is the cultural conditions that repress freedom of thought by elevating instrumental rationality to a position of dominance over philosophy (comprehensive rationality) and the legitimizing of greedy behavior over a 'free sharing' of life's goods.

At all levels of culture there is a creative urge intimating liberty and social transformation. The chains of society are felt oppressive and the mind dreams of better worlds. Authority is tested, then challenged, and finally overcome by the courage and wit of spirited persons. This scenario runs through all of human history at greatly varying levels of sophistication and self-awareness. Some changes are logical, just and truly admirable, while other revolutions are spurious, jejune, and destructive. The social transformation that seeks to overthrow repressive authority in order to forge a freer world expresses the deep need of the human mind to project and extend its values of freedom out into the concrete world. Humans clearly want freedom. Unfortunately, we are not very successful at constructively expressing our free powers in the formation of stable cultures. We tend to confuse 'freedom' with the 'personal quest for power' and 'community' with 'authoritarian groups'. It is not that we do not want freedom, but rather that we have only a vague understanding of it and consequently have great difficulty in rationally integrating our social universe around the central ideal of freedom.

In general, the people of a give culture fail to understand freedom in the following ways: 1) We lack the requisite generalizing powers of thought to universalize freedom. Thus, 'freedom' becomes only my group's concern and not a universal value. 2) We tend to try to preserve freedom by legislative and formal instruction. A contradiction to be sure, since 'freedom' is not free if it can be controlled. 3) All too often, we give in to the fear of novel and strange worlds, occasioned through the activity of the free mind, by seeking refuge in uniformity. We conform to escape the uncertainty of our precepts and ideas. This sheep-headed action confuses freedom with the world of neat, clear-cut, predictable calculations. Here, not only is freedom misunderstood, but the security, existential certitude and clarity sought for are never attained, for they are escapist illusions in these circumstances. Real security is found by learning to trust in ourselves, both as a creative process and a predictor of 'states of affairs'. We need to learn to trust our own judgment. And this requires an acceptance of fallibility, an openness to novel experience and a habit of adaptability.

The general failure to understand 'freedom' combines with our atavistic power urges and the aesthetic/ethical impoverishment of everyday life to deeply depress human freedom. Natural and cultural beauty is often hidden or disfigured by 'walls' of graffiti 'spelling out' materialism, violence, war, urbanization and 'paved parking lots' at the national park. We desperately need a pure, pristine environment of natural beauty to help reawaken our much-abused sensibilities.

The quality of the environment is very important to cultural development for a culture dominated by legislation, law and policing for its well being has already failed. Failed in being a community of rational beings. Law and order is only prophylactic against social chaos. The truth of communal life is that persons only need legal constraints in proportion to the extent that their minds are flawed and impotent. As David Hume said a long time ago, human beings who are of perfect mind do not need any laws or coercive custom. Only human imperfection can raise the possibility of legitimate legislation.

Since law and order are only, at best, 'stop-gap' measures, it is the cultivation of significant values that is eminent in cultural development. A law may be a formal effort at embodying a general truth as when justice is illuminated by legislation against exploitation of migrant workers. Yet, the sufficiency of the law, its generality and the precision of its application, are matters of common sense and wit. Just laws cannot replace understanding and generosity of spirit. We cannot coerce one another into being good and wise. We can appeal, inspire, and in the best sense of the word, 'educate' people.

We need to work toward a society where no laws or coercive customs are needed. The main conditions for the creation of such a 'far-off' and seemingly impossible 'state of affairs' is the emergence of autonomous, rational minds in the majority of the community. Since a mind develops in a world and describes a world in defining itself, the openness of an environment to creativity, reflection, and rational action is paramount for rational development. And through a growth in creative rationality and independent judgment, there can be a blooming of truly communal values.

A social environment can be destructive in at least two ways: first, by presenting destructive images of violence, materialism, and exploitation and power as though these irrational pursuits were human and noble ends. And second, by not presenting images and logical suggestions for healthy, rational ways of living. It is the questions that are never asked that indicate the social boundaries of discourse and show the conceptual regions where oppression and tyranny have walled up curiosity and rationality in a given community.

In a truly free culture, all issues and significant values would be placed out in the 'open' for public inspection, analysis, and debate. The basic assumption and governing paradigm of a culture should be subject to critical thought as well as the main ideas, policies and applications in effect at the time. The idea that the fundamental ideas and values that constitute a culture's intellectual framework cannot be questioned, but only believed as 'sacred' and 'self-evident', is a throw-back to hyper-authoritarian politics along the line of the 'divine right of kings' over their subjects. Nobody has a special 'pipeline' to God and nobody can find truth for you. Everything is open to question and logical integration in a rational scheme of discourse. Unquestioned acceptance of popular opinion, government policies, and conventional norms reduce thought to an instrumental function.

The conformist thinks it is 'logical' to have the same opinion as everybody else. 'Everybody' thinks that way because it is 'self-evident', says the conformist. Yet, rational thought begins with the questioning of 'what is'. The 'matter' of political/social opinion is not self-evident and it exists for the intellect to ground in a web of ideas that give it its logical and experiential 'place'. The conformist knows nothing of this reflective process and considers 'logic's job' done when he/she simply accedes to the relevant authority or calculates efficiently from the 'self evident' (unquestioned opinion). With the social conformist we, again, see the ugly side of instrumental rationality.

An environment where all 'issues' could be freely discussed without fear of reprisal would be an intellectual wonderland. A cultural world where the most beautiful art and thought flow lazily through the village of the mind for all to savor, only if desired from the bank of self-sufficiency, embodies the wisdom of true knowledge and learning. An economy that provides the basic needs so that people may live with leisure and cultivation in mind necessarily compliments the environment of free thought and high culture. Last, the presence of vast tracts of wilderness where people in reasonable numbers can respectfully come to enjoy and replenish their spirits promises deep satisfaction of body/mind. These environments of free thought, art, economy, and nature taken as a complimentary whole form an ideal world for contemporary persons to dwell in. Perhaps, we should consider living more in concordance with such a world? If so, we need to create that kind of world for ourselves.

The creation of an ideal society, or even a better society, requires a great effort by many different people. The sequence for positive change in a culture always begins with an idea. We are thinking beings and from our architecture of ideas comes material and social change. An idea is expressed and, perhaps quite unexpectedly, other persons transform it into definite action. The environment is transformed by the group that holds the transforming idea valuable and functional. In turn, the social changes brought about by the collective acceptance and application of the potent idea lead to new ideas with potential for novel social changes. In this way, one person's idea can become common stock, while the 'heightened awareness' of one person is woven into the fabric of a culture to produce many, diverse forms of that original sensibility and conception. Social institutions that embody freedom, beauty, and excellence suggest in many subtle ways the birth of adventurous romance and lucid idealism. However, the influential institution first requires an original idea to begin the social process that leads to their stable establishment. Thus, thought and action complement one another in a reciprocally re-affirming process of social creativity. We transform society through ideas, which are themselves transformed by the social institutions that the ideas generate and projected into concrete existence.

The environments of our contemporary Western cultures are not congenial with the lofty values of creative living, freedom for all, social justice, communal sharing and the life of reason. In order to have more humane and rational persons, we need to fashion a better environment, a 'place' where liberty, reason, and sympathy can flourish. The end is a forever receding dream of a just and peaceful community; it is what is still left to do when the generative idea has exhausted itself. In between are our cultural institutions and their influence on our minds.

People want freedom and in such a way that it leads to material prosperity and communal peace. Yet, people also fear that 'state of peace' for it leaves the ego vulnerable to trust and care for others. Destructive urges compete for dominance with the amiable feelings and reason is often hard put to keep things in order. Prosperity can lead to selfishness and, worse yet, a turn to power seeking. And the whole conflict-laden psyche functions in a world, both inner and outer, that is uncontrollable. Our controls on things are only partial and always dependent on natural conditions of body/mind and environment.

Thus, life becomes a matter of 'spiritual' development, a quest for meaning and ultimate value in life. Only by achieving a 'spiritual' peace can a contemporary person discern order and value in the universe constructed by the human mind. Social freedom, material goals, cultural values, and the processes of intellect, instinct, and social feeling require a framework to be organized within. A 'spiritual' life is the quest for an individually satisfying 'framework' for existence. Those 'born to be' thinkers turn to philosophy and seek the rationality (or lack of it) in the universe. Most people are not so inclined. So, they turn to other projects: religion, art, and the practical knowledge of interpersonal relationships. Whatever a person turns to for spiritual nourishment needs to suit the particular individual's natural potentials, while putting him/her in intimate touch with other lives and beings.

A government can be controlled by a small elite or by the will of the people. Descartes always praised the simplicity, elegance, and symmetry of constructions created by a single mind. He saw only incongruities and 'rag tag' patterns in cooperative creations. The advantage of a single creation is that the work or architecture can be shaped to the 'perfection' of a Vision. Visions, while speaking for all of us, are deeply personal in style and meaning. The common meanings and values need to be understood as emerging from a distinct personality embedded in a particular history. Something is lost of the power and purity of a Vision when many minds and hands wish to form one and the same object. So, should a social construction (government) be determined and shaped by a single mind?

Descartes' idea works well for creations where the decisions and the consequences of the decisions lay firmly on one person's shoulders. For example, the design of a beautiful building being the creation of a single architect is an ideal project to illustrate Descartes' meaning. However, when the decision-making process and the consequences are the responsibility of many, then Descartes' idea is unworkable and crude. A society consisting of the expressions, and their interactions, of many free agents cannot logically be ruled by a single mind. We cannot take responsibility for other people's decisions and aspirations. On the contrary, that is up to the individual.

In a society, where the power lies in the hands of a few, the many are subject to a 'childish state of mind'. The role of the 'many' in a governing by the 'few' is a passive, semi-conscious abdication of the power to shape and govern. 'The 'many' under such 'leadership' tend to retain a childlike dependency and naïveté in regard to authority. Since freedom and mature, autonomous activity are essential values of a healthy culture, governing by the few cannot be justified. The responsibility for civilized life is everybody's option and duty.

It is a 'duty'. We are free to reject, but if we do not participate meaningfully in governing society, then we have used our freedom against ourselves to diminish our power to create and make life 'good'.

A society can never logically force a person to participate against his/her will in any but cases where the survival of the group is dependent on such participation. The rule needs be 'to come and go' as you will. However, every effort to show the beauty and promise of a freely shared life in a harmonious community should be expressed. We are all responsible for everything that happens. Under this vast responsibility, we struggle to do what is best. We cannot force 'truth' or 'goodness', and our powers are terribly limited to change things, yet each one of us has this power, the capacity to create in a world where we live out our powers in a vast sea of communal care.

Plato's 'philosopher/king' was a grand theoretical effort to bring beauty and goodness into the everyday life of the community in so far as it lacked these chief virtues. Unlike a contemporary elitist, Plato's philosophers do not represent the 'national interest', any political party, or even the 'people'. They simply stand for an instantiation of wisdom. Thus, the philosophers, as Plato saw it, are outside of all special interests, beyond political partiality and self-interest. Their function is to turn back the inevitable tide of human irrationality and self-seeking passion through a just use of the 'divine-wisdom' that is the special concern of the philosopher.

Plato's philosopher/king is not an elite member of the ruling community. Wealth and power are clearly rejected by the philosophical ethic. Government is not to express the will of the powerful and wealthy.' Government is to embody justice, the application of reason to the 'affairs of state'. The philosopher/king is an elite only intellectually, and not in the world of status and social power.

Understood in this way, the rule of an individual (king) over a people is much different than the rule of small, elite groups over democratic societies. The difference is that the philosopher/king has no special privileges only a great responsibility to preserve the social/economic system that gives them such privilege

The problem of an elite group ruling society is not necessarily that of the inequality, injustice, and insensitivity of the fortunate 'few' to the miserable 'many'. The philosopher/king serves as an illustration. The problem here is that the wise and impartial judgment of the philosopher still excludes the all-important function of self-governing from the 'many'. Plato's hypothetical social thinker is not out to exploit any group or class, or remain complacent before poverty and ignorance. Yet, the thinking king, under Plato's scheme, cannot allow the decision-making power to be in the hands of the 'ordinary' citizens. Thus, we still have a kind of 'tyranny' here in which the ordinary citizen is treated as a child.

A culture cannot afford to have a large population of 'childish' adults for citizens. Their intellectual and moral immaturity drags the whole community downward toward the lowest common denominator. Yet, any form of political elitism, including rule of the wise, is, in principle, going to depress the participation of the ordinary citizen in the active governing of his/her society. Thus, elitism is ruled out for those of us who insist on a true political freedom, for all. The only type of 'elitism' that is acceptable, to me, is the aristocracy of the mind, which exhorts each rational individual to develop his/her mind to the utmost for the intrinsic merits and joy of doing so. Elite intellectuals can contribute novelty, reason and, at its best, socially regenerative ideas. On the other hand, 'intellectuals' who serve the practical powers of the state debase reflective thought and the freedom and well being of culture. A philosopher cannot serve any master but 'truth', and, as we know, truth is only found in an intuition of the 'perfectness' of an idea. The mandarins of society are not real philosophers, but often are servile, uncreative hacks even in the special domains (social science, political science, etc.) that breed them.

Democracy in some form allows for serious participation in the 'affairs of state and community' by the ordinary citizen. Usually it is a small population with traditional freedom and a relatively simple economy. Early 19th century New England communities would suffice as an example. The ideal, here, is leadership by the 'many' from the roots up, the grassroots political movement.

People's governments can overcome the problem of elitist control. Yet, the quality of culture in a people's, or grassroots, government depends on the mentality of the people. Democracy can become a form of tyranny by the majority. The fact that the majority of the citizens want something does not mean that their wanting it is 'good' or even useful for society. Slavery and war have at various times been quite popular with human societies. Stupidity, ignorance, and repressed hostility can be expressed through the devious masks of 'popular' and 'proper' opinion and rule. Indeed, I think it is only the traditions of freedom and spirituality that enable what little our planet has of participatory democracy to keep from sliding into the pit of banality.

The 'people' must rule because it is a necessary function of mature individuals to govern themselves. If the 'people' don't rule, the 'elite' will rule. A tyranny of some form will be the inevitable result. On the other hand, the fact that the 'people' rule guarantees nothing. A humane and just society is needed, but how can it be constructed?

❖ ❖ ❖

The political autonomy of participatory democracies could be joined to an imaginative and critical, libertarian social theory. The possible 'slide of democracy' into banality could be cancelled out by a freedom loving, life-affirming individualism in the cultural sphere, as distinct from the strictly economic and political, while a socialist concern for the material well-fare of its citizens needs to be promoted in the economic region to keep the governing section from violating its own good sense.

Various social/political arrangements can be invented to solve problems. There are probably many possible forms for a good government to take. Yet, what all the forms of government must have to be 'good' are: 1) active and significant participation by the citizens in the "affairs of state and community"; 2) intervention in economics to insure the material well-being of every citizen; and 3) non-interference in all matters of the mind and culture, except strictly governmental action.

Who should rule? We can now tentatively answer our question. It is we who should rule. Every citizen of the community freely functioning to improve the 'state of all' is what is needed for good government. However, the 'rule' of the people needs to be subject to ever-increasing waves of cultural freedom and rationality. Constitutional law and civil rights are necessary. But it is the cultivation of the mind and heart of its citizens that, in the long run, will preserve and extend humane government.

A government's justification is in its contribution to a culture's will to affirm universal freedom, rationality, uniqueness, and peace. The extent to which governments do not meet these high standards is the exact extent to which these governments need to be transformed. We are all responsible for everything and it is up to us to make our world better. As a humble beginning in that direction, I would like to turn the reader's attention to a few of my government's most serious problems: namely, communication distortion, which undermines freedom of thought, and intervention in foreign countries, which violates the rights of whole cultures. These are problems that intelligent and humane citizens will have to tackle for it is obvious that a 'wayward power' is not likely to reform itself. Modern governments obtain their 'conscience' from relentless, citizen pressure.

11
INTERVENTION
✤ ✤ ✤

If the goal is 'peace', then violence is the last, if it is allowed all, thing to be allowed. Violence from 'super powers' is often in the form of intervention. For example, the US frequently intervenes (Vietnam, Nicaragua etc.) in the political/economic life of other nations and peoples. The intervention can, and often does, involve military force.

Intervention is only logically justifiable if it preserves the life and liberty of all involved parties in a dispute. Now, since intervention with military force necessarily destroys the lives and liberty of at least some participants in a dispute, it takes an extraordinary set of circumstances to justify itself. The possible justifiable conditions for intervention are those conditions where violence can be used to decrease the total loss of life and liberty by all concerned. Such situations are those that involved violence functioning exclusively in the role of 'self-defense'. In other words, if attacked, you have the 'right' to use violence to the extent that you preserve your life and liberty, and not one bit more.

Thus, if a strong nation annihilates a weak nation, which was foolish enough to attack it, there are no grounds for justification by self-defense for the strong nation needed only to employ its vast strength for self-protection and not unleash it to destroy the enemy. 'Self-defense' means stopping the 'enemies' power to harm you without destroying the 'enemy's' capacity to function as an autonomous agent. So, the violence can only be to 'disarm' without destruction or conquest beyond the harm done in the purely defensive action of disarming. A single analogy would be that of a powerful man preventing a nasty, destructive child from harming someone by simply holding him back from his intended target. The destructive use of intervening violence would be illustrated by our analogy in a case where the powerful man beat and killed the nasty child in the name of protecting the intended 'victim'.

Military force is not easy to control, nor is its physical consequences completely predictable. However, a logical rule could provide limits and guidelines. The following rule is such: military force should be used only to increase the life and liberty of all participants in the conflict. Thus, in our 'strong man-weak child' analogy the beating and killing of the aggressive child results in the loss of liberty for one party, and the preservation of liberty for the other two combatants. While the disarming of the aggressor child, without the need of torture, killing, or permanent enslavement, results in the preservation of liberty for all the parties.

In thought that expresses concrete experience, there are generally several, varying logical inferences that can be made. Among the acceptable inferences, one can sometimes be found that is the most congenial to the leading principle guiding the deductions. For 'intervention' the inferences that work at solving problems without the use of physical force are the most cordial. The guiding principle for intervention is to preserve the life and liberty of all parties involved to the maximum. This means that problems should be resolved by cooperative discussion, compromise, and rational consensus, for in that way, no one is enslaved or killed. By contrast, the use of military force is, at best, the lesser of two evils. Peace is the ideal relationship and non-violent, rational processes for solving problems are the means to that end.

Many Americans have a false notion of the legitimacy of 'intervention'. To intervene is to 'step-into' the affairs of others so as to shape or influence their outcome. Since people are by nature free, rational beings, the choice and responsibility for acting is up to the individual and his/her 'representative' institutions. A foreign power, strictly speaking, has no business telling any other nation 'what to do' or 'how to live'! It is only in cases where self-preservation is at stake that intervention can become a logical possibility to be considered.

In cases of war, preserving the lives of citizens and the lives of the people of other governments are candidates for possible justified intervention. When a country's governing social values are inimical to our own ideals (Kuwait, Iran, China, etc.) the case for intervention falls entirely on the right to 'physical existence'. 'Liberty' is not an issue in a culture that does not have institutions embodying and articulating the value of personal freedom. To exist is everyone's 'right'. Intervention is often rationalized as being for the good of those being intervened on. The destruction of the rain-forest and its stone-age inhabitants is all for the 'good', the good of the human species, the well-being of the indigenous peoples, presumably because they can now wear shoes and work menial labor jobs instead of wandering the primeval forests, and the good of the forest (for it now has 'meaning' by serving human needs (profits). The basis of such 'thinking' is that what is good for the 'controlling/industry' is good for the planet. Of course, nobody has bothered to consult the 'forests', the indigenous human dwellers or the citizens of the countries involved in the brutal industry.

People do not exist to be controlled and fashioned to the tastes of other persons acting, legally or illegally, as authorities. Intervention, which does seek control over others, is neither rational nor good. We act for our interests, but our interests are not necessarily justifiable. 'Interests' that, in their manner of happening, negate the freedom and interests of others are not justified. For example, the Western invasion of the rain forest that drives primitive people from their homes is clearly morally wrong. The 'interests' of the logging industry denies the right, and even the 'right to have a right' to the native forest people and the organic tree life of the rain forest. Life is reduced to a practical function in service of a commercial institution. Plants and people are commodities and exploitable resources for potential economic profit. Yet, in the eyes and words of the 'exploiters, it is all one for the 'good'. In that case, the "good" is whatever makes profits for the 'company', and inversely economic profit is 'the good'. Person's who conform to the 'good equals profits' equation are noble citizens, while those who do not are ignorant, evil and certainly undesirable.

The successful functioning as an instrument in the mechanics of a profit system does not attain 'goodness'. The 'good' is the goal, only partially achieved, of self-perfection through self-awareness and freedom. Self-perfection expresses an inward satisfaction with certain possibilities for being in the world. In short, we experience 'perfection' of self when we attain a surpassing harmony with the world, both the intelligible world of thought and the sense base universe of the environment.

'Profits' is not an inward concept, rather it refers to an external result which one may take pleasure in as 'status' or 'power' feelings. The pleasure is not the satisfaction of experiencing a 'state of perfection' in things. On the contrary, 'profit' masks the nature of things and shows us only the result of our manipulation of things. There is no sense of 'perfection-in-things', for there are no independent things to relate to in the 'profit mentality', but only objects to be manipulated for utility. And a self as a free creator of satisfying relationships is not possible for the 'profit mentality'. The self is only an empty void that observes the results of the 'economic' machine's processes. Perhaps, subject to fear, pride and the pleasure of being efficient the self of the 'profit mentality' experiences only basic animal passions. Lacking is the sense of connectedness, an innate relatedness to nature and humanity that characterizes our concrete spirituality and the general grounding of our intellectual life. Thus, the reduction of the universe to a 'profit machine' excludes the possibility of obtaining a true 'goodness'; our experience of exploiting nature is only one of prolonged banality. And the pathetic and irrational attempts at justifying economic intervention and exploitation are the mind's most banal moments.

Intervention in the affairs of others is a difficult and risky project. To give counsel, aid, and labor to others may be good and noble; however the giver needs to be sharply aware of the will and wishes of those persons being 'benefited'. If they do not want help it should not be forced upon them. Even less should we impose our way of life on others. We cannot make a person good or wise. We can only provide nourishment and support for their quests. And our 'support' needs to respect and affirm the individuality and freedom of those we are supporting. Otherwise, intervention becomes a positive 'evil' confusing love with power and 'self' with ego.

12
COMMUNICATION
❖ ❖ ❖

Whenever there is a great uniformity of opinion on social/political matters in a community, then a high probability of sheep-headedness exists in that community. No idea is truly self-evident or beyond reproach from some perspective; political ideas are controversial by nature. Thus, to treat a political notion as self-evident is absurd. Yet, how often we observe uniformity of opinion in social/political discourse when the issue itself logically cries out for an analysis to review its many meanings. Cases of overwhelming consensus in social political matters are often the result of treating controversial ideas as though they were self-evident. Ideas that should be critically explored are instead accepted at face value and heedlessly projected out as certain truths. The next step often is a rush from blind ideas to aggressive action.

A logical treatment of social/political issues is bound to produce a variety of positions and ideas. People have diverse opinions because they are diverse characters with distinct interests, both cognitive and emotional, unique styles and varying abilities. Thought expresses interests, and thus, diversity. Logic does not put the rule of normalcy on life. On the contrary, it only establishes limits via consistency, criticality, and probability within which a great diversity of ideas and expression can flourish.

Uncritical and unreflective beliefs are elements in an irrational pattern of thought for the consistency, probability and accuracy of our beliefs is attained only by the integrating power of rational reflection. Thus, if we are generally unreflective about our lives and communities, then we are also going to be quite irrational—being a 'sheep' and being irrational are inseparable.

How do we know when people are not thinking independently? Conforming minds often claim to be independent in thought and word, even when they are parroting some authority. Faced with this type of deception, the usual method of getting information by asking a direct question (are you an independent thinker?) is useless. However, we investigators of culture are not stymied for we can observe the social groups of our subjects. As I mentioned, a high degree of uniformity in a community over social issues is a lucid sign of herd conformity. A healthy range of diversity of opinion needs to exist in a community before it can be justly suspected of independence of mind. Also, a high degree of agreement between leaders of different sections of society on questions of a social/political nature indicates conformity to a system, rather than diversity of opinion with agreement on certain well reasoned points. Excellence in reasoning does not produce uniformity of opinion with agreement on certain well-reasoned points. For example, we know that when leaders from institutions, as different in function as the media and the government, share a uniform view of things political that an unreflective existence prevails. Either a strict conformity to a system or a mindless collusion exists in such cases.

Another method of discerning a lack of free, critical thought in a community is to require that reasons be given for all assertions and claims of a social nature. Individual speakers need to show the 'logic' of their opinions. A truly uncritical belief will quickly find itself in contradiction with other beliefs when the relevant believer begins to rationally examine and explore his/her beliefs. For example, the all too often heard justification for military violence, 'to liberate', when the culture being liberated is fascist or the liberating agent is, itself, a highly authoritarian militaristic community.

Violence enslaves, it does not free. And when there is 'no choice" but violence for protection, the violence must be kept strictly within the limits of what is necessary for self-preservation and liberty from subjugation. The collective cry 'liberty' when fighting to establish a tyrannical government, or overthrow a tyrant by exercising a much greater tyranny over the people of the enemy is outright irrational. And its public support is on a level of a mob mentality. It is especially in cases like these when human life is on the line, that rational thought should be given free rein. A community, and each individual citizen, has the right to demand a logical justification for the actions of its government by the government that is supposed to be representing its people.

A healthy culture requires certain conditions to exist in regards to communication/interaction among its members. We need models of thought that express the self-liberation of thought from uncriticized assumptions, dogmas, and excessive reliance on techniques. A paradigm of 'reflective thought' that is both bold and rational through and through would be ideal.

A thought model for communication over social/political issues needs to consider the role of logic in discussion and argumentation. Techniques and formal procedures cannot replace natural wit and sound judgment in cognitive matters. Even excellent principles of thought and conduct can be mangled by stupid, rigid, and overly prosaic applications. Thus, reasoned scenarios of fruitful, social discourse should be understood as illustrations showing possibilities for successful communication, and also, as a set of guidelines suggesting limits to follow in the actual practice of social communicative interaction.

The 'logic' that matters in reflection on events that are concrete/experiential is dialectical, rather than formal. Formal logic splits the symbolic universe into 'universals' and 'particulars'. A 'particular' is any distinct thing that falls under one of the universal categories. For example, mortality is a general category under which anything subject to death is placed in the logical scheme. Now, it is certain that classifying objects in that manner fails to capture the diversity of individual things and the complexity of the relationship between networks of things. We need to know not only that 'X' has this property, but in what unique way 'X' has this general property and how 'X' is different and similar from other objects. In our example, 'mortality' would be quite different for a 'man' and a 'flower'. Yet there would be some similarities as well as differences, in the experience of death for both life forms. A thinker needs to preserve the uniqueness of these experiences in order to give reason its just do. We want to describe an actual world and not just a convenient one. The subtle interrelationships expressing interdependence need to be determined in our rational classification of things. Formal logic cannot preserve the diversity that the natural mind articulates, and thus is not sufficient for solving concrete social problems.

Philosophical logic is called dialectical. It differs from formal logic primarily in that it preserves the individuality of the concepts it logically organizes. In a healthy dialectic, the objects reflected upon are represented as they actually are in the mind, and the web of relationships that branch out from the reflected object are essential parts of the object being reflectively studied. For example, a musical piece (symphony) is not just a member of the set of 'artistic productions' but a unique event consisting of aesthetic, technical, mythical, cultural, and ideational experiences.

And it is the function of dialectic to synthesize all these diverse, but related, meanings into a concrete whole. Thus, dialectic is a logic of the concept. A concept is an idea expressible in words. Concepts convey specific meanings and stand to one anther as a web of mutually supporting meanings. That is, one concept is the logical grounds for another, which in turn is the logical support for another in the continual process of constructing a logical architecture. The 'architecture' has no fixed point but rather is forever creating its orderly, yet, open web.

Reason is the process of synthesizing concepts in such a way as to make the world intelligible by integrating experiences. And its method of operation is dialectic, broadly conceived as 'critical/process' thinking where each idea corrects or modifies previous ideas in a sequence of synthetical understanding.

For our social/political purpose, we only need to emphasize the importance of a thinking that is both open-minded and critical. Formal techniques, quantitative methods, and empirical data are only, at best, tools in the reflective process. It is the critical judgment of the individual reasoner that is paramount. And no 'mechanism' can successfully subvert this essential fact of human cognition and intelligibility.

In collective discussions of social problems, there is a host of knowleged problems to be avoided: 1) a tendency to rely on the opinions of authorities (editorials) or the degree of assumed popularity of an issue, when making decisions and casting votes; 2) use of academic techniques which are <u>reductionist</u> or in some other way superficial and irrelevant to the arguments with the mistaken notion that their label of science makes them true; 3) failure to be aware of essential inconsistencies in one's views and arguments and a refusal to modify views when important inconsistencies are revealed; and 4) domination of thinking by the collective interests of the group one belongs to. Thought expresses interests, but should not be controlled by social/political ambitions. That most crude error only reduces thought to an instrumental calculation of predetermined ends. We need to be open minded, relatively impartial, and imaginative in our solution and final decision in order to think effectively.

My brief list presents some of the most common problems encountered in group discussions. I leave the extension and 'fill-ins' of the list to the reader. What needs to be remembered, though, is that selfish and irrational thought and expression lead to destructive action. Somewhere on the earth, people are harmed by those who wield power in conformity to irrational dictates and policies.

The first requirement for social/political communication in a representative government is access to relevant information. If citizens are unaware of what is happening in their world, then no matter what their rational powers, little can be done. In our American culture, much of the information involving political and social issues comes from the media. If the media does not accurately present the relevant facts, and in sufficient number, the public will be uninformed. Access to the media is not a realistic option for most citizens, which creates the further problem of how an ordinary citizen is to communicate publicly. On the other hand, powerful citizens have ready access to the media, which they can try to exploit for their private interests.

In a true democracy, the function of the media should be to impartially present all the relevant facts concerning issues of public importance. The media people can have and express a viewpoint of their own, but it should be labeled a 'viewpoint' and it should be only one of many perspectives communicated. The media should not play the role of an influential power, but rather ought to function as a 'servant' of the people in its business of impartially collecting information for citizens to analyze and make decisions on.

Information is always interpreted in accordance with a framework, which expresses interest and values. In a government of the people, the interpretations have to be varied and reflect the range of opinion across society. For example, a newspaper should give equal space to all the competing viewpoints over an issue, including the least popular position. The editors can express their viewpoint, but it should receive no more print space than the competing view of dissenters. When editorials express a uniform position on an issue it is another case of sheep-headedness.

Political issues are controversial and neither the proper function of democratic journalism, nor the nature of thought allows for high degrees of uniformity. Lack of critical reasoning is no stranger to the world of journalism.

The public in democratic countries needs a forum as a public avenue through which ideas can be generated and distributed to the culture at large. Every major social/political issue should be treated as the common property of the minds of the citizens to be analyzed, argued, and resolved for the public good. All the underlying assumptions, principles and leading practices that support a policy should be brought to the forefront of the social consciousness and logically judged for worth and utility. Thus, social/political issues should be decided on the basis of a complete critique by a fully participating citizenry.

The political habit of mind that tacitly censures certain questions in order to create a limit on what can be allowed in a discussion is a slow poison to both participatory democracy and reasoning itself. The limits on discussion and argumentation should be simply the limit of the creative powers of the rational participants in the discussions. Predetermined frameworks and intellectual taboos are violative of reasoning and freedom of expression. For example, the taboo on questioning the rationality and moral right of US intervention in foreign governments and economies allows for arguments and decisions of the gravest consequences to be made without ever logically considering the rational justification and moral legitimacy of the action decided on. uch a 'state of affairs' undermines the democratic rights of the citizens.

The media presents information theatrically and in patches, a few on-the-spot shots, a terse comment, and a concluding plea. Even if the media gave the news in a free and relatively impartial manner, which I do not believe it does, it would not suffice for adequate communications of social/political events in a contemporary society. The problem is that the conventional news can only give, at best, a first taste or suggestive glimpse of current events. What remains is the, sometimes painful task of contemplating and analyzing the relevant event with an eye to action. And where are the Western institutions to aid the citizens in this endeavor? Universities as a rule are non-contentious and conservative politically. Besides, they address only a small segment of the voting population. Churches could play a role, but most churches have strong biases and a tendency to stifle creative thought, particularly of a controversial social nature. They are likely to be of help only for certain issues that don't offend their beliefs, practices, and politics. As a positive force for the general liberation of the mind and the society created by the minds of its members, it is quite unlikely to prove to be beneficial.

I think that grassroots discussion groups work well in supplementing and critiquing information given by the mainstream institutions. However, grassroots groups are sharply limited in power for the national policy is firmly embedded in the matrix of traditional capitalist leadership.

In theory, a sufficient number of sincere, grassroots political/environmental groups could transform the collective mind of a whole culture. However, this has not happened for the support systems of funding , education, regional economic independence and communal service are lacking. Combined with the hard resistance of powers to be to change in the structure of political decision-making, the lack of sufficient support systems buries the brave efforts of countless idealists and reformers. Yet, some progress is surely made. And whatever 'good' is established in the culture is due entirely to the generous courage of such groups.

It is clear that our institutions need to be reformed or recreated in order to bring true liberty, justice, and peace to contemporary social life. How that will, if indeed it does, happen, I don't know. I am not even sure what ought to be constructed and activated in the way of improving society. However, I am sure that a new means of distributing information and opinion is necessary. A means that will encourage and challenge the ordinary citizen to be critical, logical, creative and a vital participant in his or her culture's social life. The responsibility for finding a 'new' way is everybody's. The philosopher can play an important role in social reform by engaging in an intellectual archaeology that reveals the hidden structure and grounds of our culture's values, institutions and practices. The social activist can implement ideas and stimulate social change. Yet, in the end, it is the ingenuity and courage of the ordinary citizen that makes the lasting changes in our culture's ways and norms.

Humane, productive communication over social/political issues requires not only a forum for the free exchange of ideas, but the cultivation of values that embody freedom, reason, and peace. A state of mind that is congenial to free, critical, social interaction would be a great boon to a culture in search of liberation and justice. The key to creating social values in a culture is to remember that values are not behaviors to be elicited by training, but rather they are attitudes and ideas that can be learned only freely, and their values must be presented as possibilities to be rationally accepted or rejected by the autonomous individual. Learning values in this way shows the significance and wonder of human freedom.

The state of mind I am thinking of as beneficent to society consists of three overlapping regions: 1) ethical, 2) psychological, and 3) social. The moral attitude that is necessary for a humane society is such: each person is a creative participant in the universe. This power to creatively participate in the processes of the world is the central project and value of human life. Thus, it is a universal value expressing a common human nature. So, we are co-partners in a freedom and ought to act so as to respect and affirm each others' liberty. And with a little rational extension, we could accept and affirm the freedom and destiny of every life form. The inevitable conflict in trying to live this ideal requires the cultivation of good judgment and the will to 'perfect' oneself.

Good communication is cultivated by the learning of psychological knowledge that enhances interpersonal relationships. In particular, the habit of accepting others without passing judgment on their worth or trying to control their feelings and speech is valuable. This encourages freedom of expression, honesty, and open-mindedness. Also, the acceptance of your own feelings without denial or repression is cultivated in the process of developing better interpersonal relationships. This encourages honesty and flexibility of mind.

A positive 'social state of mind' sees the well being of society in the acceptance of the responsibility to act for social solidarity and in the attainment of authentic consensus. Human beings must determine their own values. So, critical discourse and the exploration of the assumptions on which political actions are based is a necessity for the social state of mind. However, this requires a high degree of critical thinking on the part of the citizen. Values and facts cannot be accepted uncritically or a true consensus will not be achieved.

A false consensus can occur when resolution of social problems is prevented by distorted communication. Distorted communication conflicts with communications aimed at attaining a rational social consensus. It intervenes in the capacity of individuals and groups to create satisfactory agreements over common problems. For example, technological science promotes economic development through its power to manipulate the physical environment. Yet, it does this by arbitrarily distinguishing facts and values. So, the desired outcomes of technological activities are ruled by the values of the efficient procedures and arbitrary goals. Arbitrary because the scientific manipulations cannot be informed by rational thought in a system that denies the function of values in rational thinking. Modern technology is simply a very efficient exploitation of nature and society according to the blind desires of an out of control, irrational power. Thus, a true consensus is out of the question under the domain of the instrumental rationality of technological science.

Since technology has pervaded into government and the economy deeply, a major problem exists for the lovers of reason and consensus. The growth of the economy is linked to technological progress and the popular mode of thinking is that of half reason, instrumental rationality. Thus, the critical road toward human values and free, consensus-based politics will require tremendous creative effort. A modest beginning is in the formation of groups to engage in critical thinking about the assumptions, policies, and actions of their governments.

REFERENCES

❖ ❖ ❖

Clarke, Thurston. *Ask Not: The Inauguration of John F. Kennedy and the Speech That Changed America*. New York: Henry Holt and Co., 2004.

Descartes, René. *The Philosophical Writings Of Descartes* in 3 vols. Cottingham, J., Stoothoff, R., Kenny, A., and Murdoch, D., trans. (Cambridge University Press, 1988).

Descartes, René. *Discourse on Method and Meditations on First Philosophy*, tr. by Donald A. Cress (Hackett, 1999).

Descartes, René. *Meditationes De Prima Philosophia/Meditations on First Philosophy* (Bilingual Edition), ed. by George Heffernan (Notre Dame, 1990).

Dostoyevski, Fyodor. The Brothers Karamozov, New York: Random House, 1995.

Jürgen Habermas. The Theory of Communicative Action, Volume 1: Reason and the Rationalization of Society (The Theory of Communicative Action, Vol 1). Boston, MA: Beacon Press (March 1, 1985).

Jürgen Habermas. Trans. Jeremy J. Shapiro. *Knowledge and Human Interests*. Cambridge, England: Polity Press, 1987.

Jane Braaten, *Habermas's Critical Theory of Society*, State University of New York Press, 1991.

Hume, David. *A Treatise of Human Nature*, edited by L. A. Selby-Bigge, 2nd ed. revised by P.H. Nidditch, Oxford: Clarendon Press, 1975.

Hume, David. *Enquiry Concerning Human Understanding*, in *Enquiries concerning Human Understanding and concerning the Principles of Morals*, edited by L. A. Selby-Bigge, 3rd edition revised by P. H. Nidditch, Oxford: Clarendon Press, 1975.

Hume, David. *An Enquiry concerning Human Understanding*, edited by Tom L. Beauchamp, Oxford/New York: Oxford University Press, 1999

E. Husserl. *Ideen II* (Nijhoff: The Hague, 1952), s. 191; also *Idees directrices pour une phenomenologie et une philiosophie phenomenologiques pure de la constitution*, Traduit par E. Escoubas (Paris: PUF, 1982);

Ideas Pertaining to a Pure Phenomenology and to a Phenomenological Philosophy, Second Book, tr. by R. Rojcewicz and A. Schuwer (Dordrecht: Kluwer Academic Publishers, 1989).

Edmund Husserl. *Ideas Pertaining to a Pure Phenomenology and to a Phenomenological Philosophy,* First Book, translated by F. Kersten, (Dordrecht: Kulwer Academic).

Kennedy, John F. Inaugural Address, Friday, January 20, 1961.

Kant, Immanuel. *Groundwork of the Metaphysics of Morals*, trans. Mary Gregor, Cambridge University Press, 1998; first published in 1996.

Kant, Immanuel. Foundations of the Metaphysics of Morals. Trans. Lewis White Beck. New York: Bobbs-Merrill, 1959.

2002 *Groundwork for the metaphysics of morals*, tr. Arnulf Zweig, edited by Thomas E. Hill, Jr. and Arnulf Zweig. Oxford; New York: Oxford University Press. ISBN 019875180X

Peirce, C.S. (1883, ed.), *Studies in Logic by Members of the Johns Hopkins University*, Little, Brown, and Company, Boston, MA, 1883. Reprinted: *Foundations of Semiotics, Volume 1*, Achim Eschbach (series ed. & pref.), Max H. Fisch (intro.), Johns Benjamins, Amsterdam, 1983.

Peirce, C.S. (1898). *Reasoning and the Logic of Things, The Cambridge Conference Lectures of 1898*, Kenneth Laine Ketner (ed., intro.) and Hilary Putnam (intro., comm.), Harvard, 1992. Text of the lectures that William James invited Peirce to give in Cambridge, MA.

Peirce, C.S. 1931-58. *The Collected Papers of Charles Sanders Peirce*, eds. C. Hartshorne, P. Weiss (Vols. 1–6) and A. Burks (Vols. 7–8). (Cambridge MA: Harvard University Press).

Plato. Trans. C. D. C. Reeve. *The Republic*. Indianapolis, Indiana: Hackett Publishing Company, Inc. 2004.

Plato. Trans. Desmond Lee. *The Republic*. Penguin Classics; 2nd edition (February 25, 2003). London, England: 2003.

Plato. Ed. John M. Cooper, and D. S. Hutchinson. *Plato Complete Works*. Hackett Publishing Company, Indianapolis, Indiana: 1997.

Porte, Joel. *Emerson in His Journals*. The Belknap Press of Harvard University Press: Boston, MA. 1982.

Strunk, William; et al (2006). *The Classics of Style*. The American Academic Press.

Thoreau, Henry David. *Civil Disobedience and Other Essays*, Dover Publications, May 20, 1993, Mineola, NY (Dover Thrift Editions)

Whicher, Stephen E. (1950). *Freedom and Fate. An Inner Life of Ralph Waldo Emerson*. University of Pennsylvania Press.

www.ingramcontent.com/pod-product-compliance
Lightning Source LLC
Chambersburg PA
CBHW060845050426
42453CB00008B/834